THE PROPERTY INVESTMENT MENTOR

CREATE PASSIVE INCOME, BUILD WEALTH AND MAKE
MONEY WORK FOR YOU AS A PROPERTY INVESTOR

CRAIG CAMPBELL

THANKFUL

I would like to take this opportunity, first of all to thank my mum for being so supportive of whatever I have chosen to do and for being such a good role model in my life.

My wife for being the amazing person she is and giving me the help and continuous support this book needed to get done.

The selfless acts of; my brother Daleyon, friends; Charles, Rowena, Joslyn and cousin Junior for taking the time out to give me valued feedback along the way.

I am so blessed to have you all and others in my life that have shown such support, I am truly Thankful.

INTRODUCTION

I have been a property investor for over 18 years and I am here to help you solve the puzzle of property investment. My original intent in creating this book was to provide a guide for members of my family and close friends. By reading this book, they will be better equipped to navigate the property market without relying on the expertise of outsiders who are often motivated by their own personal goals. I wanted those who are close to me to receive excellent advice from someone who has their best interests at heart, coupled with a wealth of experience and a proven track record of successfully investing in the property market through several differing economic climates.

After much contemplation, I realised that this book could also be of huge benefit to other people who wish to learn about property investing, to start investing or to improve their results from property investing. This realisation led me to write this book for a much wider audience. My goal is to help individuals gain more awareness about this industry and ultimately achieve their own definition of success.

One of my main objectives is to help others avoid mistakes that could stunt their growth in the property industry. When I started out, I also needed guidance so I sought the help of others but there was no one I could trust or who had the knowledge to show me the best path to take. When taking out my very first mortgage I was advised by the lender's mortgage advisor to take out an endowment mortgage based on his assessment of my appetite for risk. Endowments were described to me as a savings pot and when making mortgage payments you would pay the interest on the loan and also pay an amount in to the pot that would be invested into steadily growing shares that would pay off the mortgage quicker than a repayment mortgage under normal circumstances.

Taking out an endowment mortgage was the worst decision I could have made. Endowment products no longer exist because they were such a waste of time and money for the majority of consumers. I made monthly payments in to the policy for years and on auditing it, I ascertained that I had a lot less in the policy than I had originally put in. I would have been better off saving that money under my bed or spending it on myself because the majority just evaporated into thin air. A repayment or an interest-only mortgage would have been the better choice for me.

If I had someone with knowledge, experience, and without self-interest whom I could turn to at the time, this lesson could have been prevented. The estate agent who showed me the property was about 17 and did not know much at the time; he was just eager to get his first deal. My solicitor was not very helpful either, he was not interested in helping me to understand the process or in explaining what was happening at any point.

I just did not know what I was doing, all I knew for sure was that purchasing the property was the right move and everything else about the process was trial and error. I did not read any books on the topic and the internet was not really around at the time. It was like breaking your virginity: you know you want to do it but you're not really sure what you are doing for the first few times and then you start getting the hang of things after a while.

Seek advice from people who know what they are talking about. Some estate agents, solicitors and brokers cannot distinguish a good deal because most of them do not personally invest in property. Some are clueless about the kind of profit a property needs to earn in order to be considered a worthwhile investment.

There will be people who will discourage you because they have never invested in property themselves. Drown out their unfounded opinions with your own better judgment. It is not wise to ask someone who has never been in a relationship for girlfriend advice, right? It is better to ask someone who has been in a loving and progressive relationship for many years. Be discerning of the advice that you receive and be aware of the biases of the individual who has given you that advice.

Ideally, you need to seek counsel from someone who has similar goals to yourself, has been investing in your preferred area, and who is proactive and decisive enough to make excellent investing decisions. They can share experiences and specialist advice because they genuinely want to help you. A person who has been engaged in this industry for a number of years, who has gone through a couple of recessions, yet has still managed to make money from property investments is someone who can propel you along the right path.

You will learn about the ways to succeed in property investment in the pages of this book. Be a wise investor: learn, build your portfolio, continue educating yourself and enjoy the journey.

TABLE OF CONTENTS

Chapter 1 Mind-Set

When you take the plunge into the world of property investment, you can expect to encounter challenges ahead. Armed with the right mind-set and proper motivation, you can succeed in this industry. I have had good levels of success in life and I believe that some of these are a direct result of the principles below:

If you are doing the right thing in the right way, the results will come. If you keep the consistency going, things will happen. In a similar way to gym membership, if you have not put in the work, why would your body change?

There have been times when things were not happening according to plan but it made me dig deeper. In property deals there always seem to be some issues; I would have lost a few deals when problems came up, but instead of focussing on the problem and how unlucky I was, I focussed on the solution.

Treat people with a good level of respect and patience. Try and help them if you can as you never know when and how they may be able to help you in the future. As I write this book I am negotiating a deal that only came to me because I was advising a lady who was having some mould and tenant issues. Other people did not see the benefit of helping her but if I can help I will always try without thinking about what is in it for me. This same lady recommended me to her friend who needed a quick sale on the basis of the way I dealt with her.

Maintain your integrity and honesty during all your interactions so that you can always stand strong. By being honest you can never be caught out, you will always be perceived as genuine and people will pick up on this. Be like the teachers at school that genuinely cared about you and who wanted you to learn and thrive, rather than those that just wanted to collect their pay cheque and did not care about your education.

Always try to understand people's viewpoints when they are expressing an opinion; you are not always right and you could even learn something. If you do disagree, explain your points clearly.

If you want something you must invest the necessary time. There are no alternatives to giving a goal the time it deserves.

FOCUS ON POSSIBILITIES

Everything is possible with the right focus. The most difficult challenge in the beginning is believing in yourself and your own capacity to succeed. If you think you can do it, you most certainly can. You just need to focus on working smart and working hard in order to achieve your goals.

I remember that when I decided to buy my first property, I did not think twice, I just thought that it made better sense to purchase it rather than rent it as the price was the same either way. The monthly mortgage payments and the rent were the same, and it was the right option because if I bought it, the property would be mine. I did not even think of the equity building up and creating wealth from it at that point but renting it would just mean paying someone for something that I would never own.

My dilemma then was my financial situation. I was studying, and also working in a low paying job; however, I persevered and bought the property because I believed in its potential. It turned out to be the right decision because although I had just enough money to make it work, it was still a success. I could lie and say this was all part of my master plan and I had the foresight to know how important this first step was going to be, but I did not. This first purchase turned out to be the most important step in my property investment journey because it was this property that provided the source of funding for future deposits on subsequent properties. Had I not taken this first step the story would be very different. It was not a bed of roses as I ended up working two jobs seven days a week for over a year to make things work.

I had many friends who were against my decision. The majority of them even laughed at me - except for one who had a different view to the rest. After the laughter, they told me it was not possible because I was 20 at the time and considered to be too young to take such a risk. They even added that it was not the right time to buy property and that I should just enjoy life, parties and decide on mature things like property purchases later on in life. One friend in particular was adamant that house prices were too high and I should wait until they came down; this particular friend is still waiting for the prices to come down.

The friend who did not laugh already owned a property while the others did not. His support for my decision was based on first-hand experience not on zero knowledge. As I mentioned earlier in the introduction, listen to people who know what they are talking about.

At the time, I listened to a positive voice, my own, that believed I could make it happen; I explored all the possibilities of making it work. It was so clear to me that buying was the obvious move but the majority of my friends could not see it. I often wonder why. If you have the courage to follow your intuition and the drive to find the best strategy, go for it.

CHAPTER 2 UNDERSTAND THE INTEREST RATES

I will show you how to master the interest rate test, starting with the basics. There are currently two main types of interest that you pay on a mortgage: interest only and repayment.

When it comes to interest only, as the term implies, you are only paying the interest on the original loan every month. The loan remains outstanding at the end of the term unless you have another way of clearing the debt in full. On the other hand, repayment means that you pay the interest every month plus an extra amount that goes towards paying off the original loan amount. The good news is that after the end of the term that you have taken the mortgage (usually 25 to 35 years), the debt will be fully paid.

The interest only option is better applied to a situation where your cash flow is not in the best state and you have no long term plans for a certain property. This would be the best move for flats that you intend to sell in 5 to 20, years' time if they do not work well in your portfolio due to the service charge which may increase.

A repayment mortgage is a better option if you have excellent cash flow and you have managed to secure a competitive rating, preferably below 3%.

All things considered, my preferred suggestion would be to take out an interest only mortgage and make overpayments i.e. pay an extra amount over and above the agreed monthly payment. This gives you the power to pay up to 10% of the outstanding mortgage every year. This means that if the interest rates increase or decrease and your cash flow rises and falls, you can alter the amount of your overpayments to suit your situation. The amount of money you can save by simply making overpayments is amazing, and it is also possible on a repayment mortgage. It is about maximising your money to its full potential. Take a look at the benefit of saving your money over a few years compared to the financial benefit of making overpayments on some mortgages.

Should I take out a fixed rate or a variable rate mortgage?

Variable rate is a specialised type of interest rate charged by a lender. It fluctuates over time because it is based on an underlying rate which is normally the Bank of England's rate plus an extra percentage - 3% for example. If the Bank of England's base rate increases then your rate will also increase. Hence, if the bank base rate decreases then your mortgage payments will decrease accordingly and if interest rates increase, so will your mortgage payments. So if you are on a variable rate mortgage package, you are always vulnerable to interest rate movements.

Fixed rate does what it says on the tin. The rate you agree will be the rate of interest you pay for the duration of the period of your agreement. Therefore considering which one to choose and over what period is most important. This depends on you and your approach to risk, however, I like to think that I eliminate as much risk as I can when making these decisions.

If interest rates are high and it seems like they will keep increasing, then it would make sense to take a fixed mortgage rate product because this will protect you from any increase in your mortgage payments. Moreover, it will eliminate any uncertainty from the equation. Nonetheless I suggest that you limit the duration of this type of product to three years.

Here's a situation worth considering: a lot of people had 6.5% rates fixed for five years plus, however, the base rate dropped to a record low and most people on variable rates were far better off than those stuck on the fixed rate of 6.5%. These people would have made a lot more money from their rents had they been on a variable rate linked to the Bank of England's base rate. Most people with interest rates linked to the Bank of England's base rate have never had it so good. For instance, now in 2015 the Bank of England's base rates are low and therefore over the next few years, they might increase, however, due to the fact that I have some really low interest rate products below

2%, I do not need to be so concerned about fixing my rates. If I did not have these products, I would start looking around for some good fixed rate deals but the interest rates would have to go up by about 3% for me to be worse off. I cannot see this happening within 24 months, thus I will be better off with my low variable rates for now. This is because there is no fixed rate at present that is as low. The base rate can only go one way as it is so low and this situation will result in all lenders increasing their mortgage product interest rates.

Finding a good interest rate is essential. You should check the market at least once a year to ensure that you have the best product especially if you are not tied in to a product for a particular period. I do this every year and save myself money by finding a better rate. Certainly, this is one of the best practices I can recommend. I have managed to save myself a lot of money by doing this, but you must be aware of fees that some of the lenders charge. You should make sure that if there is a fee you still benefit, in a similar way to shopping around for car insurance and house insurance renewals. If you shop around you can save money but not every offer is as good as it may seem initially. Calculate the total cost versus the total saving; if the new product will not save you money, there is no point in moving.

If you are choosing between a fixed rate and a variable rate and the rates are very similar, it will make sense to choose the fixed rate as you will not be affected by any fluctuations in interest rates.

THE BUYING PROCESS

The buying of properties generally follows a number of key steps and stages. To give you a basic idea of the way it works, I have outlined the steps in order to help manage your expectations:

➢ Find a property that you want to buy
➢ Obtain a mortgage in principle from a lender
➢ Put your offer to an estate agent or seller
➢ The seller agrees to your offer
➢ The solicitor's details are exchanged along with the agreed price
➢ A valuation is instructed
➢ The solicitor performs his searches and reviews all legal papers connected to the property
➢ A mortgage offer is received
➢ Enquiries may be raised by the buyer's solicitor and the seller's solicitor will respond
➢ Results from searches are well received
➢ Pay your deposit to your solicitor
➢ The buyer and seller exchange contracts
➢ More enquiries are raised and answered

- ➢ The completion date is agreed between all stakeholders
- ➢ Monies are requested from the lender by the solicitor
- ➢ Completion takes place
- ➢ Collect the keys to your new property.

How to Save Money to Buy Property

First Step

This goes back to the principles highlighted by the book "The Richest Man in Babylon" and more recently the book "Rich Dad Poor Dad". The basic rule is to ensure that you put a share of the money you are currently making aside in to a savings account. The recommendation is 10% to 30% of your overall income. For example, if you are paid £1,000 a month, try and save £200, and arrange for this money to be debited from your account automatically. You can set up a standing order that transfers this money in to an account for which you have no cash card and which may take about 24 hours to make a withdrawal. Out of sight, out of mind is the way to go.

Second Step

Perhaps my accounting background is taking charge of the financial aspect of my life but every month I get my bank statements, I enter my income and expenditures in to a spreadsheet, which has become a habit through the years. The income side may not show too many surprises but the expenditure side reflects opportunities where I can reduce my outgoings. First of all, when you see the total of what you spend each month on take away food, for example, it makes you think twice. Also, when you are spending £10 here and £10 there, it does not seem like a lot but once you add this up over the month, it really does stack up. When you look at your bank account, you will probably see a few big transactions such as accommodation, food, shopping and insurance, but look closely and you will see that the vast majority of debits are just small amounts which accumulate, more often than not, catching you off guard. The famous saying "Look after the pennies and the pounds will look after themselves," is apt in this scenario.

There is very little you can do about your accommodation costs and insurance apart from shopping around when it comes to renewals. However, you can instantly save yourself money by cutting back on the small but frequent expenditures.

After a few months of analysing your monthly spend, you will start to see if you have done well with your money in a month or if you have been wasteful. Frequent cash withdrawals of £20, £30 and £40 over the month add up to a big portion of your disposable cash. Try and use your debit card when spending so that you can keep track of your expenditures. It would also help if you make a note in your spreadsheet about what the cash was used for. It will be easier to make the decision to have leftovers for lunch when you see that you have spent £200 a month just on lunch. I know you may not have the number of transactions that warrant a spreadsheet but you can assess your spending habits when you identify patterns and areas where you can improve. I have saved money just by noticing I was making duplicate payments of home insurance and boiler insurance for example. It really does happen, especially if you are not paying full attention.

Allocating yourself a monthly budget for things outside of core bills like rent, mortgage, insurance etc. is also really helpful. I am sure you know someone who has told you that they are broke and can't come on holiday but then in the next breath mention they have savings of a reasonable amount, but these savings are not counted because they are for a new car or tuition or for a rainy day. The same principle applies when saving money to purchase your property; some sacrifices have to be made. You have to go without certain things and you will survive without them for sure. Too many people expect to have whatever they want and do everything they feel like doing without making some sacrifices. Determine your priorities and stick to the plan. Consider things like clubbing, clothes shopping, spa days, regular salon treatments, and such like as luxuries. Serious investors recognise they can minimise or do without these things to achieve a longer term goal.

What is the Yield and Why is it Important?

The yield is the total cash flow from a property in one year expressed as a percentage of the cost of that property.

Let us take as an example a property that cost £165,000 generating a monthly rent of £1000. The yield would be calculated as £12,000 (one year's income)/£165,000 = 7.2%. This will help you choose between properties when deciding on investments, you can compare them to see which one will give you the best yield. Rental income expressed as a percentage of the cost is a good indicator of the value of an investment opportunity. You must also take into account outgoings such as a service charge and ground rent: reduce your rental income calculation by the annual cost associated with the property to show the "true" or "net" yield.

Another phrase that is used constantly is "loan to value". This is simply the amount borrowed or outstanding to the lender expressed as a percentage of the current value of the property. So if a property is valued at £100,000 and you need a 20% deposit, the loan to value

(£80,000/£100,000) would be 80%. Banks do not lend above 85% currently on buy to let mortgages so as a beginner you would need to find 20% of the property purchase price plus:

Legal costs: £300-£1500

Stamp duty: i.e. 2% of purchase prices ranging from £125,000- £250,000

£250,000-£925,000= 5%

£925,000- £1,500,000 = 10%

£1,500,000 and over = 10%

Surveyor fees: from £0- £1000

Broker fees: 0- 3% of purchase price

Mortgage arrangement fees 0-3% of loan value

Maintaining a high credit rating is important because it shows your credibility and accountability. It is also beneficial if you are venturing into the realm of investments. Many doors of opportunity open when you maintain a good credit score especially when buying properties. Treat your credit file with respect as it can be the difference between making a profit or making a loss on the purchase of a property. If you do not have a good credit rating, you will not be able to get the best financial products available such as the lowest interest rates or optimal loan to value. If you have a poor credit file you may be eligible only for a mortgage from lenders who specialise in lending to people who do not have a good credit history; they charge around 3% or so more than conventional high street lenders. This will increase your mortgage payment expenses and reduce your cash flow.

I use to work for a company which gave its staff members a store card each that entitled employees to a 25% discount on all products. I used to clear the card when I was paid and did not use it that often. One day, a card bill arrived with an £8.50 minimum payment; I decided to ignore it even after they called me. I told them I would sort it out when I came back from holiday. By the time I returned, I had a county court judgment letter asking me to settle in 30 days or there would be a judgement. I could have paid the bill in full but was busy with other priorities.

Six months later, I was in the process of buying another property; everything was going smoothly. I was waiting on my mortgage decision to learn whether I met the criteria. I had paid the store card and settled the judgement months beforehand, however, the lender wrote back to advise that there was an outstanding debt against my name and a county court judgment.

I only had access to a limited number of lenders as a result. I had to go through all my important documents to try and prove that I had settled the store card. It involved contacting the court and the company I used to work for in order to provide the necessary documents. It is not a process that I would want to repeat again; hence I am now more careful about my credit rating and the responsibilities related to it.

The moral of the story is to protect your credit file like you would the monies in your bank account. Your credit record forms a substantial factor when the government, financial institutions and even car companies are deciding if you are fit for a loan, bank financing, lower interest rates, etc. There are several benefits of having a high credit score which you can take advantage of especially in the field of investments, so it is best to stay on top of your financial records.

THINGS YOU CAN DO TO PROTECT YOUR CREDIT FILE;

- Always set up a standing order/direct debit to pay the minimum payment in case you forget to pay the bill. This will avoid any late payment records building up.
- Pay all debts on time even if it's just the minimum payment.

- Try and avoid just paying the interest on credit cards or small loans; get rid of them ASAP.
- Check your credit file at least once a year to make sure there are no adverse records.
- Be disciplined with your credit cards, try not to use them to buy liabilities or things you do not need!

BUILDING YOUR TEAM

In property investment, you will be dealing with many people who can help you to succeed. It is important to share a similar goal with your broker and solicitor. Let them know upfront about the benefits of forging an alliance with you. Here are a few factors worth considering when you deal with your team.

BROKER

Select a broker who has been recommended to you by someone who owns a few properties and has used the broker on numerous occasions. You need to know the broker's capacity and to do this you must check their track record first. Preferably, the broker should also be an investor or someone who is independent and fully understands the needs of investors. Their role is to find you the best mortgage deals that best suits your personal situation and complete the application on your behalf. They are able to do this because they should know the lender's criteria along with insights gained through relationships and familiarity with lenders.

The broker must have his finger on the pulse of the market. They must be a professional who has an excellent work ethic, meaning that they do what they say they will do at the time they say they will do it. Honesty is paramount because if your broker is involved in suspect transactions, it could affect you in the future by your association with him and you do not need that kind of headache. Surround yourself with people who are trustworthy, starting with your broker.

Irrespective of your broker's quality and credentials, always check the market yourself every so often to make sure you are getting the best deals. You have to remain in control even if you are already delegating some tasks to others. As I have explained before, the only person who genuinely has your best interest at heart is you!

Tell your broker what you are trying to achieve and ask how they can help you achieve it. You can catch a glimpse of their capacity through the strategy they will present to you. You need to be on the same page as your broker so that your professional relationship can grow. I have used a few brokers in my time so I know that it is difficult to find the right person. I also chose not to use a broker on a number of occasions when I was able to find deals that were not available to brokers but very beneficial to the end user. My preference is to use a good broker because they can save you time and money if they are really good.

SOLICITOR

Hire a solicitor who has a good reputation, preferably a branded, well-known high street one. This helps when you are discussing deals, as the person may be wondering if you are genuine. However, when you make them aware that your solicitors are the best in the area, this will help to build trust. Thus, you are establishing your own credibility as an investor by hiring a solicitor, or people in general, with impeccable reputations.

What are your goals? Make sure the solicitor understands what you are trying to achieve. Let them know you may require them to do blind exchanges and act very quickly. You should make it clear that you are prepared to pay a little extra for this.

Invest in long-lasting professional relationships and let each person you work with know the benefits of providing excellent service, such as repeat business and recommendations to other buyers/investors.

MENTORS

Everyone needs a great mentor, someone who you can look to for guidance or even just to act as a role model. In the field of investments, it is good to have a mentor who will propel you in the right direction. It could be a parent who is also involved in property investment and who has achieved success. Since this person has extensive experience and a positive outlook when it comes to investments, they can be a great source of knowledge to you. It is priceless to have someone whom you see as a successful investor in the industry mentoring you, even if your mentor only acts as someone to bounce ideas off, reinforce your thoughts or challenge your opinions.

Listen to your mentor's advice but do not follow what they say unless it resonates with you. Make sure the ideas presented to you make sense so that you can decide on your next move based on them. Some of the people we consider as mentors are not always right for that role. The best teachers make mistakes, too; the sooner you realise that, the sooner you will become more attuned to your personal abilities as a well-informed investor.

CONTINUOUS LEARNING AND DEVELOPMENT

Your goal is to move forward in this industry and that entails developing your skills and strategies continuously. Go to some of the reasonably priced or free seminars and see if you can pick up any new ideas to improve your understanding of certain areas like rent to rent. You always need to innovate and move with the times, keeping abreast of major changes such as tax laws, health and safety regulations, etc. In addition, you can expand your professional circle by attending training events and seminars; knowing more people who are on the same wavelength as you can lead indirectly to more success.

You are already learning by reading this book but my advice is to continue enhancing your skills by reading more books and articles about this venture you have chosen to operate. Have a look at some of the popular YouTube videos about property investing.

Getting Started with Little Money

Being surrounded by people who give plenty of excuses for not investing can have a negative impact on the aspiring yet faint-hearted investor. You can be discouraged when people tell you that you do not have enough money to invest but there are ways to remedy the situation.

First Option

When you have few funds, it is not easy to become an investor in the property market, so buying from family members can be the best option.

Currently parent(s) can give their children a gifted deposit in respect of equity in the property which means that the children do not have to find the deposit themselves.

You should be able to get some of the deposit built in to the deal using the following illustration:

Market value is	£120,000
Parent(s) want	£96,000
80% LTV mortgage	£96,000

Determine whether the surveyor is going to agree with your estimated sale value. If they do, your seller gets the amount they want and you have a smaller deposit or possibly no deposit if it all goes according to the plan illustrated above.

However, if the surveyor does not agree to the original price by a large margin you will know that the property was overpriced to start with. This means you will need to renegotiate based on this independent valuation. An undervaluation does not help your cash position.

The transaction would be completed in the same way as a normal sale except the deposit is covered by a gift from mum and dad in the way of the property's equity.

"Help to Buy" initiatives. Find out all you can about your local schemes and put yourself in a position where you meet the criteria, allowing you to buy using the government's help with the deposit. Halfway through writing this book I asked my younger brother to read it through and give me his opinion. He told me that he was not aware of any government incentives in Canada, but after reading this chapter he did some research and he is now on a list to receive help through a government incentive that helps citizens who work for the government to buy their own homes. Regardless of where you live, please do your research.

The most important thing is to start! Yes, you may not make any money on the property or it may not be below market value but you are finally on the property ladder. What is certain is that anyone you know who purchased a property over 10 years ago now owns property that is worth significantly more than the initial purchase price.

I remember speaking to a lady named Maureen in 1999, who was several years older than I, a little while after I had purchased my first two-bed maisonette. I told her that I had paid £48,000 for it and this was a good price because the owner had died. She told me that she had paid £5,000 for her three-bed house in the nicest part of Leytonstone 20 years or so prior. This highlighted that the real magic in property investment was inflation. That is what turns a property that was once purchased for £5,000 in the 1970s to be worth £900,000 in 2015. That is beyond amazing! As I said, I paid £48,000 in 1998 and at the time of writing in (2015) the property is worth £255,000.

I believe in holding on to the good properties in your portfolio because of the magic of inflation. The magic is that once you get started and time passes, equity is built up in the property and this will allow you to buy more properties in the future. This is due to equity becoming your source of funding for future projects without the need for financing deposits.

The most important thing is getting on to the property ladder without putting yourself in to a position where you cannot afford to live or pay your mortgage.

THIRD OPTION

If your earnings multiples are not enough, ask a friend or relative to be the second person on the mortgage. You may not be able to meet the lending criteria by yourself or have enough deposit, so a joint venture may be the route forward, but please make sure it is with someone with whom you can do business in the long-term.

Chapter 4 What Properties to Buy

Are you ready to purchase properties to begin your investment venture? You need to know the type of properties to buy first: you can choose between freehold or leasehold properties. Let's discuss these two options.

Freehold Properties

Nothing is better than complete ownership and freehold properties are the best examples of that. They are definitely the kind of properties that you should aim for, because they belong to you. Not only do you own the properties but also the land they stand on. That is the upside. The downside is that these properties cost more than leasehold properties, assuming they are in a similar area. The other factors to consider are the condition and size of the property and the land where it is situated.

When it comes to the rental side, you do not always receive a premium when renting a freehold property over leasehold. If you are investing, then you have to pay significantly more for a two-bed freehold house compared to a two-bed leasehold flat. If your objective is to increase your cash flow then choosing the leasehold property should be the better option based on net yields and return on investment. Leaseholds cost less and can produce the same rent on a like-for-like basis.

LEASEHOLD PROPERTIES

You own leasehold properties for the duration of the lease thus it is very important that you buy properties with the longest lease possible.

You do have the option to renew the lease at a cost which usually varies depending on the unexpired time on the lease therefore, the less time remaining, the more expensive it is to renew. This is because the freeholder of the property knows that if you do not renew, and it runs down to zero, they can take back ownership or resell the property at market with a new lease.

Most banks will not lend on a property with a lease under 70 years due to the loss in value of the property as a result of a short lease. The length of a lease can vary with some being as long as 999 years with a £6 per annum ground rent and no service charge. I consider this to be virtually freehold. However, these will be more expensive than the more common lease that starts at 125 years. Leasehold properties usually have service charges and ground rent. Service charges are collected for the upkeep of the block/buildings and for cleaning and repairs of the communal areas such as stairways and gardens. These properties normally have a cyclical maintenance schedule which can be every 5, 7 or 10 years. The freeholder will notify you of the schedule of works to be carried out during that period. You could receive a bill for service charges that include changing the windows, lifts or even for fitting a new roof. These costs can run in to thousands. An average service charge can range from £20 to £300 per calendar month. Ground rent is a regular payment that is made by the lease holder to the freeholder of the property. The amount is determined in the lease agreement and is usually a lot less than service charges, ranging from £2 - £600 per annum.

The benefit of buying a leasehold property is the comparatively lower price, therefore over the short to medium term you will usually generate more profit each month with a leasehold property compared to a freehold. This is because you would buy the property for significantly less yet you may be able to charge the same amount of rent as the equivalent freehold property. Thus, the returns on investments are higher and, the cash flow and yield will be better. However, it is important to remember that with freehold properties capital growth will be higher ultimately.

In every situation you should always start with the maths and then weigh up the pros and cons based on your own strategy. A two bed property would be a good place start, it works for; couples, couples with one child or two children, it also works for shares or if you wanted to live there and just rent out a room. Because it is suitable for so many different rental combinations generally it is the most sought after. As we all know if there is high demand it is less likely to remain empty and you are more likely to achieve a good rent.

Ideally, buy something to which you can add value, either a property that is undervalued or a property that will be in very high demand.

Something to which you can add value is a property that is poorly laid out and therefore not attractive to buyers. A property with land to the side and a garage that can be developed in order to make the house bigger and more attractive is a good option to investigate.

The golden rule is to buy the property with the profit already in it. This is because you are buying it below market value for a number of reasons or because no one has been able to identify that the property has actually been undervalued.

PRICE

Of course, price is the most important criteria of all. If you buy at the right price, you are well on the way to making a profit but you can still lose if the structure falls down the next day - which is highly unlikely. Simply stated, if you have done your due diligence and you buy the property below market value, then it is a win for you.

LOCATION

Location is only the second most important factor when buying properties because if you are buying a property so low priced that it gives you great cash flow, and it is in high demand, who cares where it is?

The problem here is when the price cannot be considered a real bargain. In this case, the location needs to be perfect. This is going to be an investment, so potential tenants want to commute and to be close to local amenities. Hospitals, banks, schools and other important institutions should be close by. The property should also be in a safe neighbourhood where the tenants' children can roam and play without parents constantly fearing for their safety.

When you are considering the location of the property, keep in mind that everyone wants to live in a nice house within a great environment. No one who has options would choose to live on the sixth floor of a tower block with no lift. Imagine how you would cope if you lived there and IF you would want to live there.

In property investment, you should think like a buyer or a tenant frequently. Put yourself in the buyer's shoes; consider how you would want your house to be and how you would want it to appear. You are part of your target market.

Renovations and Repairs

Are there a lot of costly changes required such as a kitchen and a bathroom? Take a closer look at the flat or house that you are interested in. Are you ready to spend money on the necessary renovations and repairs? If it is only a matter of minor decorating to spruce up the place then you can deal with that. There are numerous ways to make properties look great without spending too much money. You can shop for inexpensive decorators to make the property appear and feel more conducive to happy living for its occupants.

Nonetheless, not every structural adjustment is easy to deal with unless you have access to people whom you can trust to help you fix or repair the property. Minor plumbing leaks can worsen to an extent that will cost you more money. I would advise you to stay away from properties with subsidence and extreme damp. The only way you should get involved in such projects is if the deal is so good that you can pay the best people to fix it and still make a good profit. You must take in to account all worst case scenarios because renovations and repairs can deliver many surprises, and you may not have the resources to manage them.

In summary, try to purchase long leases with low ground rents and service charges or buy freeholds. Buy properties that have a good, sound structure and are built from good quality materials. You will find borrowing difficult if the structures are not built properly as most lenders do not like to lend on properties that are not constructed from conventional materials. This will become a problem when you are trying to sell as you may be restricted to cash buyers who are willing to take the risk of buying properties that are not made of high quality materials. Cash buyers will be looking for a discount which may not fall in line with the kind of profit you wish to make.

KEY POINTS:

> Invest in properties that are built using conventional standards.

> Find properties that are located in safe and accessible areas.

> Assess a property to make sure it requires only limited work, keeping renovation or repair costs as low as possible.

> Check that properties don't need major works which could cost a lot of money.

Minor repairs and inexpensive decorating ideas are the saving grace of some properties to make them more appealing to potential buyers and tenants.

BUYING OFF-PLAN OR NEW BUILDS

A lot of people buy properties off-plan or new builds well over the market value. Because these properties are new they sometimes command a premium, but more often than not, these premiums are exaggerated and unsubstantiated. Some of these properties have been intentionally inflated and it is already too late by the time you realise this fact. Make sure you do sufficient due diligence when purchasing these types of apartments/flats.

KNOW YOUR MARKET

Investors tend to buy property in areas outside of London without doing adequate due diligence because it seems cheaper compared to London prices. It is essential to have some knowledge of the area you choose to buy in especially outside of London in the less desirable areas as they are less forgiving. An investor I know purchased properties in a less-than-ideal area in the north of England because they seemed like a good deal price wise; however, it turned out to be one of the worst areas to buy in. To make matters worse, on the first day of owning the property, boilers and copper piping were stolen. There were also issues with persistent rent arrears from tenants. Ten years later, the property is still worth less than they paid and it is empty because of tenant issues. The key is to know your market. Most of my experience is in London but I do know that a lot of investors have made money and have huge portfolios outside of London. You need to know the market and apply correct strategies to these markets.

You must know the area yourself or seek advice from someone who is familiar with the area. Make sure he does not have any vested interest in order to receive an unbiased opinion.

Some people become emotional when they are investing but the property needs to be treated as an investment vehicle which should give you a return, capital and positive cash flow. The colour of the door or wallpaper should not have an impact on your purchasing decision as people decorate properties according to personal preference. If your target market is Local Housing Allowance tenants in a socially deprived area, you do not need to install real oak flooring and top-end modern amenities. The benefits of all that effort are not enough to warrant all the hard work. You will not receive the extra financial compensation you think you deserve.

DUE DILIGENCE

How do you calculate whether you are getting a good deal on a property?

The first move would be to make it easy for yourself, by making over 7% profit in cash flow/ yield, while taking into consideration all costs associated with the property.

If you are unsure whether you are getting a good deal irrespective of price there are a few things you need to do:

Check the *Right Move website* in order to get a comparison. Check the site for properties that are similar to the one you are looking at. Follow the same process on *Zoopla*, *Net House Prices* and the *Land Registry*. This will give you a better idea of available property and the prices they are selling for in the same area. It is important to look at the recently sold properties for prices that have been achieved as opposed to asking prices which can be simply a vendor's dream or an overzealous estate agent's false promise.

Net House Prices and *the Land Registry* are the best places for actual sold prices although *Right Move* and *Zoopla* each have a section on their sites dealing with sold prices.

Speaking to local agents and soliciting their views on the potential of a property is a wise move but you should make clear the benefit of sharing their knowledge with you. What is in it for them? Tell them you intend to use the properties to rent or that you intend to sell after you have renovated, i.e. something to feed their self-interest.

The Interest Rate Test

Whenever I am purchasing a property, I always use an interest rate of 6% to calculate whether this property will be a good investment. I see 6% as a realistic representation of current rates and I have been using it in my calculations for many years. As time goes by rates will change, but the principle of using an interest rate a couple of percentage points above the average variable or fixed rate that is generally available to borrowers will still be valid. This 6% interest rate is not the best rate currently but it is also not the worst. This tells me that if times get tough and we have an interest rate increase, my investment has some protection built in, so I need not be too worried.

If a property is projected to provide a good cash flow at a 6% interest rate, that is when I can recognise that this particular investment is sound. For a while now, borrowers with good credit files have been able to achieve a 6% rate. This simply means that unless anything major happens, you can rest assured that your investment will be a good addition to your portfolio.

Some people take a more optimistic approach, using the lowest interest rate available for their calculations and then worry when there is movement in the rates after purchasing. This does not sound like a very good investment especially if your cash flows are just covering the mortgage with the low interest rate. This optimistic approach floundered in 2007/08 when a lot of people were topping up their mortgages by small amounts, which then turned in to larger amounts when things got tough. Some investors had no financial buffer and could not cope in the tough times; many properties were repossessed.

Illustration

Ideal situation: If you are buying a house that costs £200,000 using a 6% interest rate mortgage, you will be paying £12,000 pa and therefore £1,000 PCM. The rent you achieve should be £1,350. You will be making a clear £350 during bad times which is already the worst case scenario. If you are buying with cash flow as a priority, this is how you need to operate - or do your calculations using an even higher rate.

I always do this calculation on every property that I purchase in order to benefit from the cash which is in most if not all of them.

Long Term View

Property can be a short term investment. You can make money by flipping i.e. buying a property below market value, renovating it to add value, then selling it within a short period of time. I will go in to more detail on the subject in another chapter; however, the real wealth in the property industry comes from long term investment. Your actions will depend on your goals for the future. I plan to leave a property portfolio to my children so they will have a better start in life than I did. Hopefully, this kind of mindset and investment culture will progress from this generation of my family and beyond. I originally only used to think of myself and the benefits to me, but now I feel it is important to find a balance between personal current benefits and benefits for your children, grandchildren and their children too. Such a long term view can help you ignore some of the short term distractions, like get-rich-quick schemes and it can also help to improve your decision making skills overall. Hence my strategy is always to invest in properties that give me a balance of positive net cash flow combined with capital growth.

There is no such thing as a zero investment risk which is why you should consider all of your options before settling on a property. As a newcomer in the industry or even if you have been investing for a long time, a new property still needs to be assessed carefully before you decide to buy. You can listen to the predictions of many experts but there is no guarantee they will be fool-proof and accurate until the sale is complete and the market settles. It is important to pay attention to the trends and keep abreast of the developments in property investment so that you will always have an idea of what you could do next. The most important thing is to try and build in a buffer, so that if changes suddenly occur in the industry you have access to cash to cover you in the tough times. Changes could include sudden rises in interest rates or government policies to cap rents.

Preparation is important in this kind of business. You should study the market carefully and follow your instincts. The industry is competitive so you need to be on the lookout for properties constantly. Be wary, but also be a little bit of a risk-taker so you will profit from your investments. If you are not careful, you are bound to lose both opportunities and money.

My opinion is that property is definitely a long term investment and I will explain why in the following chapters.

CHAPTER 5 STRATEGIES

There are two main strategies in property ventures: the first one is to flip and the second is to buy and keep.

FLIP

This strategy involves finding a property that is selling under market value or has some potential to add value and sell it on for a profit in the short to medium term. This is a difficult task as costs can escalate dramatically, or there could be a sudden downturn in the market which reduces the property value.

The downside to this is that you no longer have an asset increasing in value over time. You also need to pay tax on the profit depending on your situation. If you have made this property your main residence for a few years, profit on its sale will not be taxed, but if you have purchased it as a straight investment opportunity, you are subject to Capital Gains Tax.

Any property can be flipped once the figures stack up. Flipping is good for a variety of reasons, such as;

Raising cash to purchase a better yielding property,

Improving loan-to-value ratios to protect the portfolio,

Building up cash reserves for tough times,

Shedding poor performing properties and properties that you do not want in your long term portfolio based on the costs of renewing the lease or the high service charge.

However, once you have sold and the monies are in your bank any issues regarding downturn

in the market, interest rate hikes or tenants' rent arrears have no impact on you.

BUY AND KEEP

This is my personal favourite! Again, look for the properties with the most potential below market value or the ones that only require a small deposit. With buy and keep, you never sell. No matter what happens, prices keep going up over the long term so what is the point of selling it?

A COMMON MISTAKE TO AVOID

Some investors buy a property purely for the capital growth. This is fine if you have loads of disposable income and the cash flow is not an issue because you are investing in a prime location which should see significant appreciation in the future. On the other hand, if your cash flow is not stable and the property does not give you a profit/positive net cash flow, you will need to supplement the costs with your own money in order to pay the mortgage each month; I refer to this as a 'top-up'. This is not a desirable situation to be in. If you acquire a few 'top-up' properties and the interest rate starts to increase, even one tenant who stops paying their rent could see you facing repossession very quickly. I believe that you should buy properties which provide income and which cover all associated costs. There should not be any top-ups!

If you do need cash, you can simply re-mortgage on the basis that the tenant in the property will be covering the mortgage. The positive cash flow will be giving you a monthly income and if you ever want to buy that one, special expensive item for yourself, you can ask your current lender for a re-mortgage based on the excess equity and the loan-to-value ratio which is usually limited to 75-80% (meaning you must leave 20-25% of the overall property value as equity). Thus, I believe it is not necessary to sell because you can still have the money by releasing equity, which has the bonus of non-liability for Capital Gains Tax.

Yes, you do have to pay interest on the extra monies but this is being paid for by the tenant while the asset is appreciating at the same time. Wait a while and you will be able to go back to the lender and generate more monies from the same property because the value has increased which means there is more equity in the property.

When you sell, that's it! You can't get the property back.

As previously stated I believe in leaving something for my children, assets that they can benefit from and in turn leave for their own children makes sense to me.

Leaving money to your family is good but inflation erodes the value of money whilst it increases the value of property. I remember the times when a bus ride was 10p and chips were 35p, but due to inflation and other factors, bus fares are now £2 and a portion of chips is approximately £1.50. So if your family leaves you money it is likely that it will be able to buy you less and less as inflation increases and time passes by. Property prices usually rise with inflation, outperforming inflation in the long run and definitely outperforming cash.

CREATE A PORTFOLIO

Your portfolio is your asset as a property investor. You need to start building it carefully through a solid investment strategy. You can buy properties that will generate cash flow especially if your current financial situation is just above average. You should satisfy yourself that you can minimise the risk and gain profit from your first property investment.

If you already own a home, then you can check the equity of your own property and use it to buy the first property in your portfolio. Equity is the difference between the amount you owe the bank and the value of your home. You can discuss this with your bank or other mortgage lenders and learn about your loan options by using your equity as security.

Once you purchase a property, you can choose to sell it or rent out so that you can buy your next property and so on. You need to strike a balance with the contents of your portfolio. You may want to start with a small buy-to-let residential property once you have some valuable experience behind you. You can explore larger high yielding investment type properties such as a house of multiple occupancy, commercial and developments. Get feedback from friends and family regarding the properties they favour.

How to Multiply Your Portfolio

Before you proceed further, recognise that this is not a get-rich-quick affair!

Currently, the rules reveal that you can generally re-mortgage after six months of owning a property. However, most lenders will not lend more than 75% to 80% on a property and will also apply a stress test to ensure you meet their criteria.

The rental income also has to be above 125% of the mortgage. For example, if the mortgage payment is £100, the rent has to be £125 each month. The secret is to buy property with equity at the start or realise the equity by adding value as discussed earlier. If you do not have these options, be prepared because the process will take a little longer.

Once the six month period has passed, you can get your property re-valued and assess whether the value has increased enough to release equity. See the illustration below:

Purchase price	£100,000
Initial deposit	£25,000
Mortgage	£75,000

This represents a loan to value of 75% (£75, 0000 / £100, 000) which is what most lenders currently lend on average against buy-to-let products.

After a minimum of six months you will be in a position to re-mortgage and release equity; however, this may have to be done over a much longer period depending on the degree that house prices have increased over the period or the discount you achieved when purchasing.

Market value   £175,000

Mortgage   £75,000

Equity   £100,000

Loan to value   £75,000 / £175,000 = 42.8%

You can ask your lender for more money as long as the rent covers 125% of the new mortgage. In addition:

Market value   £175,000

Re mortgage   £130,000

Equity   £45,000

Loan to value   £ 130,000/£175,000 = 74.2%

Cash in the bank for a deposit to buy a new property would be £55,000

This is how to make your money work for you; if you have more than one property and you have purchased correctly your operation will work more efficiently.

This process is then repeated but the secret again is buying the right property and not liquidising all of the equity. It is also important to have back up equity and it is imperative that the property will give you good positive cash flow. A lot of people recommend yields of 10% and 8% but if that returns a cash flow of £50 a month, is the investment really worth it when it could actually cost £50 in petrol to visit the property a few times in a month? Common sense must be applied when taking yield, cash flow and all other factors in to consideration. Leave yourself a margin of error, some level of buffer is required for contingency if rents fall or interest rates increase.

I have never purchased at auction myself, because the property has always been sold above what I felt was a reasonable price to complement my strategy. However, from my experience I would say that you should be extra cautious because there is a reason why the property is being auctioned. Sometimes the seller just wants a quick sale without the hassle or the time that a traditional estate agent sale could take. Another reason could be that the bank has repossessed the property from an owner who has not kept up with his/her mortgage payments.

Generally properties for sale at auction are those with issues that deter the average investor or end user from purchasing the property quickly. These types of properties usually would not sell so quickly on the open market due to some of the following reasons:

Not mortgage-worthy because it does not meet most lenders' criteria of having a kitchen and bathroom.

The structure may have issues such as subsidence or it may not be constructed from traditional materials.

The length of the lease may be very short.

Certainly deals can be found through auctions but be very careful as a lot of people get caught up in the hype and excitement of an auction and end up paying too much.

In September 2015 I attended an auction where I placed a bid on a property that only had 20 years left on the lease but had everything else going for it. I visited the property and did my due diligence to ascertain what the value should be if it had a good lease and was in good condition. All the evidence told me that the property would be worth around £230,000. My local solicitor made me aware that he had recently completed a lease extension of a similar property owned by the same freeholder; it had cost around £110,000 which made sense as the guide price was about £50,000. However, during the auction I met with other investors that had turned up for the same property. We had a quick chat that revealed they too were aware that the renewal of the lease would be above £100,000. The property sold for just under £200,000 and I questioned myself as to whether I had missed a trick here so, I approached the person who had won the bid to find out. I met an excitable gentleman who explained that the lease renewal would only cost about £5,000. I asked if he had done any research to validate the estimated cost of the lease renewal and he said he had not but this is what he thought it should cost. I had renewed a lease previously that had 60 years remaining that cost more than £18,000 in the same area of North London and was confident that this gentleman had an unpleasant surprise ahead of him.

There are many situations to prepare for if you are engaged in property investments. You can encounter banks ready to repossess a potential customer's home or even your own property unless you do something about it. I am going to share a few of the ways you can stop this from happening and how you can benefit.

If possible pay all the arrears off. However, I understand you would not be in this position if this were an option, especially if you are the owner of the house. Try to borrow money from friends and family first.

As an investor you would first agree on a fair price for a quick sale. Secondly, you must exchange without doing any searches and with the minimum deposit if you need to exchange within 48 hours. The solicitor will do some quick checks on the land registry for example but essentially you are prepared to take the risk because of the discount you are getting by moving so quickly and stopping the repossession. The key is to put down the absolute minimum deposit. On a number of occasions, this has been as little as £1 to a max of £1,000. The next step is to apply to the court for the repossession to be postponed on the basis that the property will be sold imminently. The mortgage lender will not be worse off with this delay and the seller will be better off.

For this to work, you need to have two solicitors (yours and the seller's) who are prepared to work fast and secure the mortgage from the get-go because the court may only give you a short period of time to complete the sale.

Why should the seller give you a discount in the first place?

Because you will stop the repossession from happening. If the property is repossessed, this will affect the owner's credit file for at least six years. They will not be able to purchase another property or pass a credit check to rent a new property in the future. Things will be very difficult for them going forward.

The seller would also run the risk of having to pay more for the property in the future. To explain further, if the property is sold in an auction below the price necessary to clear the amount owed to the lender, the seller will still have to pay off the balance even though they no longer own the property. They are at the mercy of the auction or of the asset management company whose agent may also sell the property for less than the outstanding mortgage.

Distressed sellers are those who are motivated to sell for a variety of reasons such as mortgage arrears, divorces or any issue that requires selling the property urgently to avoid a more difficult situation.

Building your property portfolio can be a great adventure if you can dabble in marketing. You can find distressed sellers everywhere if you know where to look. Market conditions play a major role in determining the level of creativity you need to employ in order to find people who will sell their property for a discount.

Since you are testing the waters, you can try these options:

Distribute leaflets in areas where you want to invest: door-to-door is one option or advertising in a local paper.

Go to county courts when they are conducting repossession cases - distribute your leaflet and tell them that you are a local investor who can stop the repossession. These people have few options and most are ready to sell. They want a fast and convenient transaction.

Social media e.g. Facebook, Twitter, Instagram, WhatsApp - tell everyone you know that you are a legitimate buyer and that you can buy fast at a fair price.

Send text messages to all your contacts: make them aware that you are looking to buy.

Start an e-mail campaign, and send e-mails to all your contacts.

Website Search Engine Optimisation - generate traffic to your website.

Google Pay-Per-Click (PPC) ads.

Buy lists from data brokers (It can be difficult to get a good quality list) detailing home owners who are facing financial difficulty: contact them to discover if they are thinking of selling.

Use property sources that may have good deals from people who need to sell quickly and will give a discount for a quick sale.

Check out estate agents who have properties that need to be sold quickly below market value.

There are many unconventional ways to find distressed sellers and the availability of these options is not restricted to expert investors, you can also explore them on your own. Try to observe the most important factor of all, human nature. Ask yourself what motivates people to sell quickly, or what are the desperate times in life that force people to sell a property?

Divorce is messy and everyone knows this. Spouses split up and often avoid lengthy exposure to each other by having their lawyers do the talking. In order to make the division of assets easier, their goal is just to sell their conjugal properties as soon as possible. The proceeds from these sales can be split between them so they can move on with their lives more conveniently. This is not the best scenario to strike a business deal but it can turn out to be a profitable opportunity if you play your cards right.

Never sell is my simple advice. However, if selling helps you to purchase a better yielding property with more equity and capital growth, then it may make sound business sense for you. Otherwise, the best time to sell is when the economy is strong and employment is high. If people are making more money, there is a lot of confidence in the market. Around this time there will be a lot of potential buyers. The mind-set is positive and everyone is afraid that the prices will continue increasing, and therefore it is vital that they buy immediately before the prices soar out of their financial reach.

These circumstances present the best time to sell your property. A market with lots of buyers and very few sellers will increase prices dramatically. In these times it is very difficult to find a bargain because of the media and the general optimism. The scarcity of good properties combined with limited space in the city for new properties to be built, creates favourable conditions for sellers.

CHAPTER 7 HOW TO VET TENANTS

There are various conventional methods of looking for tenants. You can post ads on *Gum Tree/Loot*, or if you prefer a more modern approach, you can use social media to advertise online. It is easy to find tenants; the difficulty lies in finding good ones. Listed below are some tips to make the process less complex and more manageable. I always recommend the use of letting agents.

First of all consider the basics. Ask prospective tenants to produce the following:

Two previous landlord references.

Current ID, passport, driving license.

Proof of affordability – bank statement, employment reference.

One month's rent and the equivalent of one month's rent as a month's deposit.

Secondly, you need guarantors and guaranteed rent insurance.

Thirdly, you should meet all interested parties and make sure you are aware of any issues that need to be addressed immediately. Establish your rules at the beginning so that the tenants are informed of your expectations. You can use the first meeting to gauge how well you can communicate with the tenant.

If the tenants are difficult at these early stages then you can ascertain the reasons why. Place the emphasis on communication, and use this time to assess the personality of your tenants. One tactic I use is to present myself as a friend or staff member of the "very busy landlord" who happens to be away at the moment. When people know you are the landlord, they can get jealous or over-familiar later and act up. You can often manage them better if you present yourself as the mediator.

This technique has proven to be helpful and effective. By putting a middle man in the equation, I have negotiated with tenants about the way they should leave the property, appearing impartial while protecting my own best interests.

You can also ask the prospective tenant if you can visit the property they are living in currently to assess how they are keeping it, this will help you to decide if they are suitable tenants. If they refuse, this indicates that they may have something to hide and that they do not take care of their accommodation to a reasonable standard. Experience has shown me that people who are open to the request usually live well and will look after your property accordingly.

DEALING WITH DIFFICULT TENANTS

I am sharing with you the three steps to take when dealing with bad tenants:

1.Communicate.

2.Communicate.

3.Communicate.

Communication is so important that it needs to be repeated three times. Before taking any action, try to ascertain the real issue. People often say they want to leave because the house is not being maintained but upon digging deeper, underlying issues are often revealed.

An example of this was a tenant of mine who was kicking up a fuss and refusing to pay rent. After further consultation, it became apparent that his recent unemployment was the root cause of his frustrations. He could not afford to pay the rent.

If there is a genuine issue, always seek to rectify it quickly. Any sort of maintenance issue regardless of its size or severity should be resolved. Landlords who do not address legitimate tenant issues can easily transform good tenants in to difficult tenants.

Once you have addressed the genuine issues but you still do not feel the relationship is one worth maintaining, then you should serve **a Section Twenty One notice**, which is a legal requirement for them to leave; this requires you to give the tenant a two-month notice to end the tenancy.

A **Section Eight eviction notice** can be used for a variety of reasons but rent arrears is the most likely reason. Section Eight has fourteen grounds under which you can evict a tenant, eight of which give a mandatory right for you to gain possession and six of which are at the discretion of the judge if served properly.

If the judge agrees that you have given the two-week notice required under Section Eight (Ground Eight) and served it correctly, he/she has no option but to grant you a possession order stating that the tenant has fourteen days to leave the property. This procedure differs all over the world so I will not go in to too much detail.

CHAPTER 8 TAX

I am not a tax accountant so this chapter is going to be very short and general. For tax advice please seek professional help. However I would like to inform everyone who is reading this book to pay the right tax. A lot of people feel that by simply getting their tenants to pay them the rent each month in cash will eliminate any chances of the tax authorities finding out that you have an investment property and you are receiving income from it. This is not the case because the tax authorities have various ways of discovering this information via reports from your solicitors on purchase of the property. In addition, the council and estate agents have to provide details of landlords and the properties they own and the rents paid to them.

Many people have a fear that the tax authorities will take all the profit, however if there is no profit there is no tax to pay and even if there is a small profit there is an even a smaller amount of tax to pay. However by trying to avoid paying the right amount of tax, you can end up making the situation much worse than if you had paid the correct amount in the first place. The penalties that tax authorities can enforce can be harsh.

Please remember that you only pay tax on the profit not the entire rent and you can reduce the profit by;

Estate agents fees,

Repair costs,

Insurance,

Ground rent and service charges,

Educational courses on property,

Telephone calls,

Petrol,

And so much more.

CONCLUSION

At the beginning of this book, I mentioned focusing on possibilities and that my mindset has been my guiding force. If you have a solid grasp of your investment strategy and the goals that you want to achieve, the possibility of your success in this field is high. Try to explore your options at the start but continue to grow and stick to your niche. I have always preferred high yields with good potential for capital growth hence my patience in holding on to properties with promising future returns. Make sure you have the buffer of a positive cash flow and capital growth to protect you when difficult times come.

Some of the basic principles of life such as honesty, courage and integrity can be applied to the field of property investment. Being honest with yourself and believing that you can attain your goals in the future is also vital. Naturally, you will be facing risks but you should be brave enough to erase your doubts and push forward. Working with a cooperative team whose goals coincide with your own is a necessity in order to succeed in this business.

There are very few businesses where you invest 15-25% of your money and as a result control what happens in 100% of the business/property. Regardless of your investment percentage in a property, the bank gives you the balance of the money, but you get the benefits of 100% of the money. This investment is about making money work for you especially when you start building your portfolio and releasing equity, **as you are simply taking money at one rate of return and using it to produce higher returns elsewhere, thus making money work harder for you than you are working for it.**

The best aspect of this business is that you make money while you are sleeping! Set up your portfolio as I have previously described, making money each month from the rent. You can place it in the hands of a very capable Estate Agent who can deal with every issue that comes along; all you do is monitor the monies being paid in to your account. Hence in this type of business you can choose to be "hands off", travelling the world for as long as you want.

There are a number of landlords/ property investors who have moved all over the world, allowing estate agents to deal with everything for them while still earning good money each month. They may receive a few emails asking for authorisation over the year but that is it. Passive income is definitely the way forward for me, as I want to spend more time with my family, rather than getting involved with managing my portfolio. There are very few businesses where you have this type of flexibility. Again, this is allowing money to work for you rather than you working hard for it, in exchange for time you will never get back.

An entrepreneurial mindset will get you far in this industry. If you are someone who constantly wants to learn how to develop, improve and grow, then you are in the right place. The most important thing is to invest in yourself and take action. The only thing stopping you from achieving what you want is you!

You say you will start something but you do not have enough time however when you calculate how much TV you have watched, the time is there in abundance or the time you have wasted recovering from too many hangovers. You may be that person who fails to invest in yourself by not buying that book or paying for a course that could help you on your journey but you have no problem buying a bottle when you are out partying with your friends. Do not get me wrong I have been that person who has purchased bottles of drink in the club and slept in the next day. So my point is to strike a balance because most people will buy Champagne but will never buy the book and wonder why they are not progressing when they have not invested in themselves.

If you take anything away from this book, I want it to be action; if you are thinking about purchasing a property in which to live or to let stop thinking about it and take action. There is no perfect time to buy and no perfect property. Better you do it today and start learning the lesson sooner rather than wait ten years and start learning then. Take action!!!!

Craig Campbell is a qualified accountant and a member of the Association of Chartered Certified Accountants. He ventured into property investments, discovering ways to work hard for money AND eventually allow his money to work even harder for him. Equipped with extensive experience in property investment, he believes that positive cash flow is essential. The concept that cash is indeed king has revealed a valuable strategy to use in the industry; he has seen profitable businesses fail time and time again due to poor cash flow. Craig has proven that positive cash flow is one of the foundations of a successful property investor and he is ready to share this knowledge with the world in relevant ways.

For eight thriving years, Craig has been the owner and manager of an estate agency based in North London. The company deals with sales and lettings as well as managing hundreds of landlord's portfolios. He manages his own portfolio and holds a certificate from the National Federation of Property Professionals, a respected awarding body in residential letting and property management. Making his first purchase in 1998, Craig has built an exceptional cash-flow-positive portfolio with amazing capital growth. One of its strengths is its recession-proof characteristic. Through the years, Craig has given valuable advice to numerous people who are interested in property investment. On a number of occasions, he has helped investors and owners avoid the pain of repossession. Nowadays, he is committed to teaching people about investing properly; he wrote this book as a major step in this direction.

FINAL POINT

If you have any further questions on property investments please email me at: craig@thepropertyinvestmentmentor.com or call me on: 02078594329

Printed in Great Britain
by Amazon

74401504R00061